First Facts®

ANCIENT EGYPT

KING TUT'S TOMB

BY AMANDA DOERING TOURVILLE

Consultant:
Leo Depuydt
Professor, Department of Egyptology
and Ancient Western Asian Studies
Brown University
Providence, Rhode Island

Capstone
press®

Mankato, Minnesota

First Facts are published by Capstone Press,
151 Good Counsel Drive, P.O. Box 669, Mankato, Minnesota 56002.
www.capstonepress.com

Library of Congress Cataloging-in-Publication Data
Tourville, Amanda Doering, 1980–
  King Tut's tomb / by Amanda Doering Tourville.
    p. cm. — (First facts. Ancient Egypt)
  Summary: "Describes the discovery of Tutankhamun's tomb and the current study of Tut's
mummy" — Provided by publisher.
  Includes bibliographical references and index.
  ISBN-13: 978-1-4296-1918-9 (hardcover)
  ISBN-10: 1-4296-1918-X (hardcover)
  1. Tutankhamun, King of Egypt — Tomb — Juvenile literature. I. Title. II. Series.
DT87.5.T66 2009
932'.014 — dc22   2007050645

Editorial Credits

Jennifer Besel, editor; Alison Thiele, designer; Wanda Winch, photo researcher

Photo Credits

AP Images/Ben Curtis, 1; AP Images/Saedi Press, 18–19; Art Resource, N.Y./ Francois Guenet, 8–9; Art
Resource, N.Y./Scala, 6 (chest); Capstone Press/Karon Dubke, 21; Getty Images Inc./AFP/Ben Curtis, 4–5;
Getty Images Inc./The Bridgeman Art Library, 14–15; Getty Images Inc./Hulton Archive, 10–11; Getty
Images Inc./Robert Harding, 11 (game); Getty Images Inc./Time & Life Pictures/Mansell, 16–17; Griffith
Institute, University of Oxford, 20; Mary Evans Picture Library, 13; Shutterstock/Maugli, 15 (mask);
Shutterstock/YKh, background throughout book; SuperStock, Inc./SuperStock, cover, 6–7

Essential content terms are bold and are defined at the bottom of the page where they first appear.

1 2 3 4 5 6 13 12 11 10 09 08

TABLE OF CONTENTS

THE BOY KING

Most 9-year-olds aren't in charge of much. But more than 3,000 years ago, Tutankhamun was a pharaoh. He was in charge of a country. The boy king isn't famous for ruling Egypt, though. King Tut is known for what he left behind. His remains have given scientists a look inside ancient Egypt.

pharaoh: a king in ancient Egypt

ANCIENT EGYPT

The time in history called ancient Egypt began around 3000 BC, about 5,000 years ago. It ended in 30 BC, when Rome took over Egypt.

the mummy
of King Tut

chest that held
Tut's organs

MAKING A MUMMY

Ancient Egyptians believed in life after death. They thought the dead needed their bodies. After he died, priests **mummified** King Tut. They took out his organs. They filled his body with salt to dry it out. Then they wrapped his body with cloth. Finally, priests placed him in a **tomb**.

mummify: to preserve a body for a long time

tomb: a room for holding a dead body

DISCOVER!

Some of King Tut's organs were saved in a small chest. This chest was put in his tomb.

TOMB ROBBERS

King Tut was buried with treasures. Furniture, jewelry, and statues were put in the tomb. Robbers broke into his tomb twice. They stole much of the jewelry. Officials closed the tomb again. It then stayed closed for more than 3,000 years.

inside King Tut's tomb

9

LOOKING FOR KING TUT

Archaeologists searched for tombs in Egypt's Valley of the Kings. By the 1900s, many tombs had been found. But they had not found Tut's. An Englishman named Lord Carnarvon wanted to find it. He hired Howard Carter. Carter's job was to find Tut's tomb.

archaeologist: a person who studies the past by digging up old objects

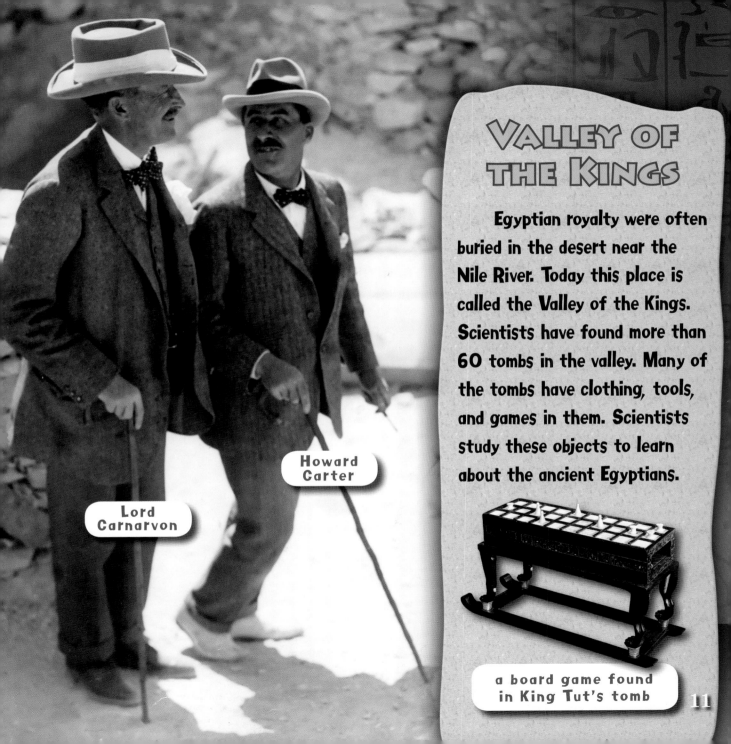

Lord
Carnarvon

Howard
Carter

VALLEY OF THE KINGS

Egyptian royalty were often buried in the desert near the Nile River. Today this place is called the Valley of the Kings. Scientists have found more than 60 tombs in the valley. Many of the tombs have clothing, tools, and games in them. Scientists study these objects to learn about the ancient Egyptians.

a board game found in King Tut's tomb

11

THE DISCOVERY

For years Carter searched for Tut's tomb. Then in 1922, he uncovered stone steps in the sand. Workers cleared the area and found a door. Carter made a hole in the door. Through the hole, he saw piles of gold objects. He had found Tut's tomb.

DISCOVER!

Carnarvon wanted Carter to give up the search. The discovery happened on Carter's last try.

TUT'S TREASURES

Inside the tomb were four rooms filled with treasures. Gold furniture and statues were piled up to the ceiling. But the greatest treasure was King Tut himself. The king's body was safe inside three nested coffins. The third coffin was made of solid gold. Over Tut's face was a gold pharaoh mask.

DISCOVER!

More than 5,000 objects were discovered in the tomb.

THE AFTERLIFE

Ancient Egyptians believed their pharaohs needed everyday things after death. Scientists found model boats, food, and walking sticks buried with Tut. These items were left for Tut to use in the afterlife.

15

DISCOVER!

Stories say Carnarvon's dog died at the same time he did. Some believed that was proof of a curse.

THE MUMMY'S CURSE

Shortly after Tut's tomb was found, Lord Carnarvon died. Many people believed he died from a **mummy's curse**.

But Carnarvon died from an infection. There was no curse. Carter continued to study Tut's **artifacts**. He lived to be 65 years old.

mummy's curse: an evil spell people believed would kill anyone who disturbed a mummy

artifact: an object that was made or used long ago

How Did King Tut Die?

Tut died young. Scientists once thought he was murdered. In 2005, scientists scanned Tut's mummy. The tests showed he might have died from an infection.

The discovery of King Tut's tomb was a major find. Scientists still study what he left behind. His mummy and treasures hold the secrets of ancient Egypt.

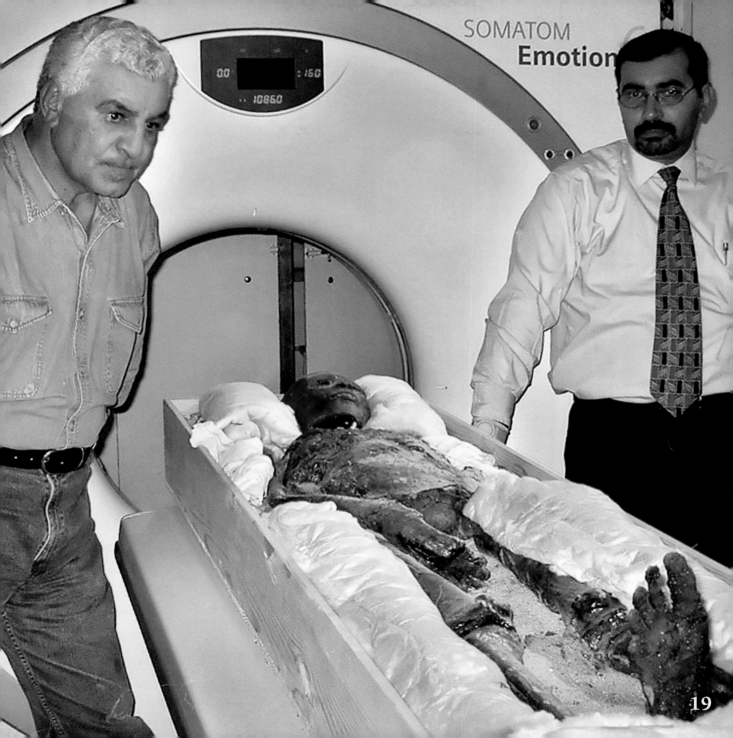

Two other mummies were found in Tut's tomb. These mummies were babies who had died at birth. Scientists studied the mummies. They believe the babies were King Tut's daughters.

HANDS ON: PHARAOH MASK

You can make and decorate your own pharaoh mask. It won't be made of gold, but you'll feel like a king of ancient Egypt.

What You Need

- pencil
- poster board
- scissors
- newspapers
- different colored paints
- paint brushes
- black marker
- string

What You Do

1. Have an adult draw the outline of your face on the poster board. Then draw in details like your eyes and mouth.

2. With the scissors, carefully cut out the mask. Have an adult help cut out the eyes and breathing holes for the nose and mouth.

3. Lay out newspapers to cover your work space.

4. Paint your mask. Once it is dry, you can go over the details of the face with a black marker.

5. Have an adult poke holes on both sides of the mask and thread the string through the holes. Then tie the mask in place on your head.

Glossary

archaeologist (ar-kee-OL-uh-jist) — a person who learns about the past by digging up old buildings or objects and studying them

artifact (AR-tuh-fakt) — an object made or used by people in the past

mummify (MUH-mih-fy) — to preserve a body with special salts and cloth to make it last for a very long time

mummy's curse (MUH-meez KURSS) — an evil spell that is meant to harm someone who disturbs a mummy

pharaoh (FAIR-oh) — a king of ancient Egypt

tomb (TOOM) — a grave, room, or building used to hold a dead body

READ MORE

Benduhn, Tea. *Ancient Egypt*. Life Long Ago. Milwaukee: Weekly Reader Early Learning Library, 2007.

Morley, Jacqueline, and John James. *Inside the Tomb of Tutankhamun*. New York: Enchanted Lion Books, 2005.

Nardo, Don. *King Tut's Tomb*. Wonders of the World. San Diego: KidHaven Press, 2005.

INTERNET SITES

FactHound offers a safe, fun way to find Internet sites related to this book. All of the sites on FactHound have been researched by our staff.

Here's how:
1. Visit *www.facthound.com*
2. Choose your grade level.
3. Type in this book ID **142961918X** for age-appropriate sites. You may also browse subjects by clicking on letters, or by clicking on pictures and words.
4. Click on the **Fetch It** button.

FactHound will fetch the best sites for you!

Index